ART I: UNIT THREE
DESIGN PERSONALITY

W9-AWP-489

CONTENTS

Author: **Keith Rosko, B.S./M.A.**

Editor: Alan Christopherson, M.S.
                          Annette M. Walker, B.S.

Illustrators: Keith Rosko, B.S./M.A.
                          Lauren Durain, A.S.T.
                          Laura Miller
                          Alpha Omega Graphics

Alpha Omega Publications®

804 N. 2nd Ave. E., Rock Rapids, IA 51246-1759
© MM by Alpha Omega Publications, Inc. All rights reserved.
LIFEPAC is a registered trademark of Alpha Omega Publications, Inc.

All trademarks and/or service marks referenced in this material are the property of their respective owners. Alpha Omega Publications, Inc. makes no claim of ownership to any trademarks and/or service marks other than their own and their affiliates', and makes no claim of affiliation to any companies whose trademarks may be listed in this material, other than their own.

INTRODUCTION

This Unit has two purposes, although these two purposes are very often closely related. Part one deals with design personality and part two with idea and concept generation techniques.

Design personality is a term artists and designers use to describe the process of self expression or communicating with others through art. Since most art is a means to express one's ideas and feelings, and a means to communicate with others, the language of design personality is very important.

Graphic design and advertising, as well as applied arts, are about communicating ideas. In most cases, an idea or concept is already present at the beginning of the creative process. Some fine arts, including painting, drawing, sculpture and so on, are more dependent on personal performance. The artist may know what they are trying to express,

but not how. Perhaps the urge to create is there, but the idea of what to create is not. In these situations techniques to develop ideas are integral to the creative process.

Creative thinking is a skill that can be applied to our daily lives. Creative thinking and problem solving skills make living easier.

OBJECTIVE

Read these objectives. The objectives tell you what you will be able to do when you have successfully completed this Unit.

When you have finished this Unit, you will be able to:

1. Demonstrate an understanding of how design can be effectively used to communicate.

2. List techniques that can be used to help generate ideas.

3. Demonstrate problem solving skills and creative thinking techniques.

In the space provided below, write what you think you will learn from this Unit, what you would like to learn, and why you are interested in this topic.

_____

_____

_____

_____

_____

_____

_____

Note: All vocabulary words in this Unit appear in **boldface** the first time they are used. If you are unsure of the meaning when you are reading, study the definitions given.

For this Unit you will need to purchase a small bottle of India ink to use in the activities at the end of the Unit.

There is also a sheet of graph paper to tear out. When placed under your paper you can see the grid through the paper. This can be used as a guide when working with the grid activities.

• •

I. DESIGN PERSONALITY

The basis for design personality is very similar to the idea of color psychology. We associate certain shapes and textures with a specific mood, atmosphere, or sensation. Why? This question has a long and complex answer which has been the cause of endless argument. It is important for the artist to learn to manipulate the associations of those who view their work and thus evoke a mood, feeling or idea. In doing so, the artist helps people better understand what is being said.

Often, it is hard to believe that as different as people are, we all have common associations, such as, black representing evil. This activity should help illustrate the point.

An **analog** is something which is similar, or analogous to, something else (thus the term *analogy*). Analogical thinking is the ability to see the similarities between seemingly different things. It is analogical thinking that allows this language of design personality to exist.

On the following page, you will see a series of nine boxes, each labeled with a word that describes an abstract concept. Using a pencil, illustrate or describe these concepts, <u>without</u> the use of repre-

sentational subject matter. For example, if the word is *love*, you must create a drawing depicting love without using commonly associated **symbols** such as hearts, people, cupids or arrows. You may not use words, just a variety of textures, values, lines and shading that can be created with your pencil. Sound tough? It's not as difficult as you might think. The key is to relax, not think too much and just let the pencil do the work. It also helps if you really concentrate on the meaning of the word.

You will also find several extra pages. Remove these and challenge other people you know to do the same activity.

The work should be spontaneous, so put a two-to-three minute time limit on each box.

This activity may put pressure on, so don't get frustrated if you can't think of anything at first. (That's the idea!). Just keep the pencil moving in contact with the paper.

ANALOG DRAWINGS

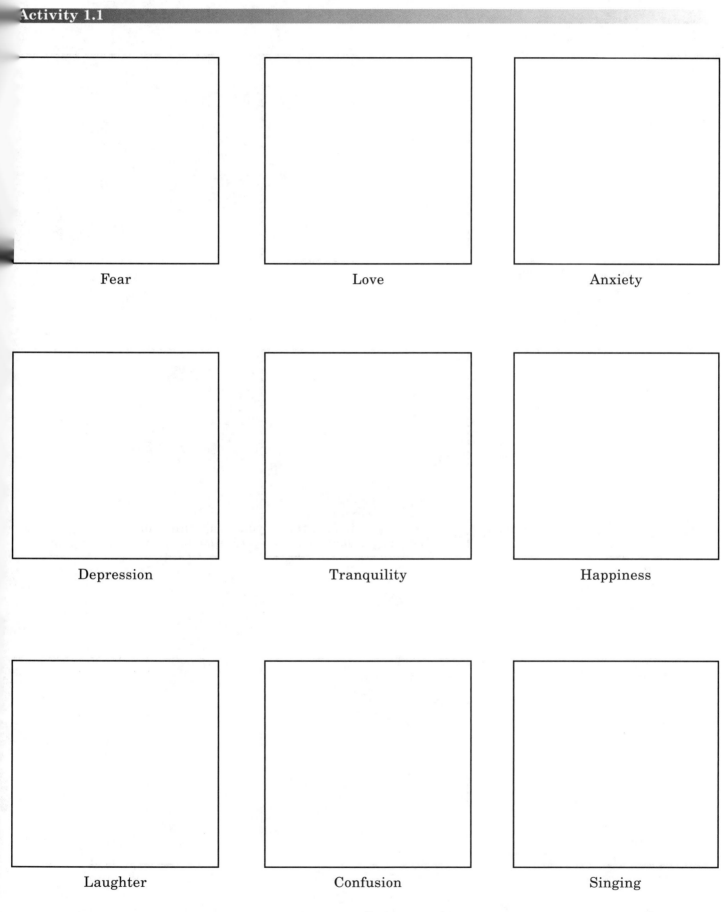

Fear

Love

Anxiety

Depression

Tranquility

Happiness

Laughter

Confusion

Singing

ANALOG DRAWINGS

Fear

Love

Anxiety

Depression

Tranquility

Happiness

Laughter

Confusion

Singing

ANALOG DRAWINGS

Fear

Love

Anxiety

Depression

Tranquility

Happiness

Laughter

Confusion

Singing

ANALOG DRAWINGS

Fear

Love

Anxiety

Depression

Tranquility

Happiness

Laughter

Confusion

Singing

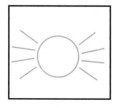

Kiss

Kiss

Kiss

Bully picking
on a small
child

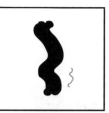

Bully picking
on a small
child

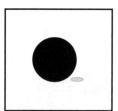

Bully picking
on a small
child

Upset stomach

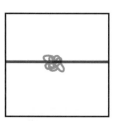

Upset stomach

Upset stomach

Joy

Joy

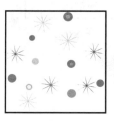

Joy

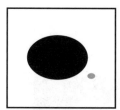

Headache

Headache

Headache

Anxiety

Anxiety

Anxiety

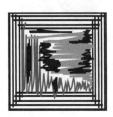

Depression

Depression

Depression

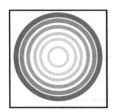

Peace

Peace

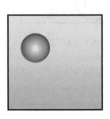

Peace

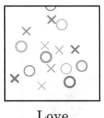

Love

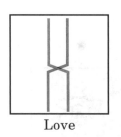

Love

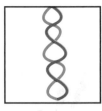

Love

Take the two previous analog sheets and look at them together. Compare the squares with those on this page. You will see that while no two are identical, (probably not identical) there are certain similarities. By looking for these similarities and defining them artists have created a visual language. The language of design personalities. Design personality begins with manipulation of the elements of design: shape, line, texture and color which we covered in the second Unit. Now, let's look at the others.

LINE—There are many different types of lines, each having its own special association.

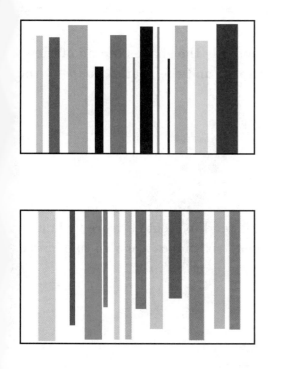

Vertical lines tend to create a feeling of stress or tension and strength. Lines that rise towards the sky tend to be uplifting, like tall trees, high cliffs or the towers of the great cathedrals reaching towards heaven.

Lines that drop toward the ground usually create an equally strong feeling of oppression or pressure because they exert downward pressure.

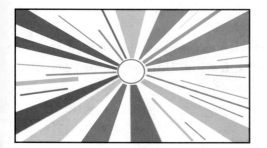

Diagonal and curved lines tend to create the illusion of movement and speed. They can help to create the feeling of energy and excitement in a design.

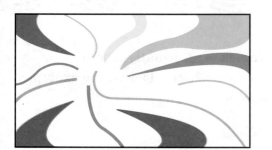

This feeling is accentuated when the lines grow in width from narrow to thicker. Curved lines that radiate have a very different look than radiating straight lines.

When working with lines you need to be aware of the fact that when a line becomes too thick it begins to resemble a shape.

Horizontal lines tend to create a more relaxed or static feeling, much like a person lying down.

SHAPE—Shape also can have quite a bit of impact on your design, not only the shapes in and of themselves, but the shapes created by your use of negative and positive space and the overall shape of the design.

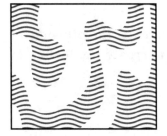

Sharp, jagged or highly angular shapes tend to create a more violent or energetic feeling. Hard-edged and geometric shapes are also considered more masculine in feeling.

The same basic design, using more curvilinear and smooth-edged shapes creates a more relaxed, much less tense feeling. Curved shapes are also usually considered more feminine in nature.

Curved shapes and lines are also more organic in appearance. It is rare to find **geometric** shapes or hard edges in nature. Geometric or hard edged shapes and angles are usually thought of as **organic** or man made. Take a look at the examples on the following page.

Look at the examples below and on the next page to see how the lines and shapes are used. How do they show mood or communicate?

ILLUSTRATION FROM *BERNIE WRIGHTSON'S FRANKENSTEIN*, BOOK BY MARY SHELLEY

Museum of Modern Art, New York.

VINCENT VAN GOGH'S *STARRY NIGHT* (1889).

Below are several examples of non-representational design that has been altered in an attempt to show or communicate an idea or personality. In the empty squares in row two, draw an object and try to manipulate the parts to express the personality listed.

	Feminine	Masculine	Organic

	Feminine	Masculine	Organic

	Feminine	Masculine	Organic

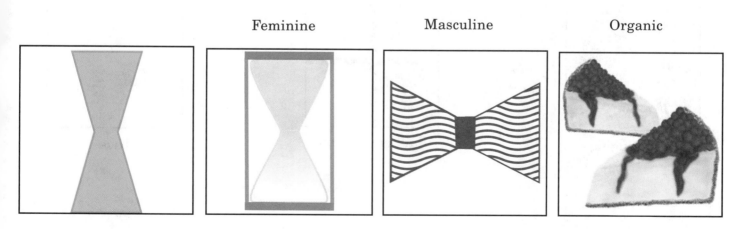

13

In this activity, you will be using shape and line only to help communicate abstract ideas or concepts. You must imagine the idea, using what you know about design personality along with your own inner feelings, attempt to create a non-representational image that will communicate the idea. Some examples are shown on this page to give some ideas how to proceed.

Mother & Child

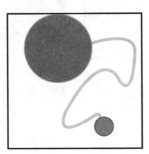

Mother & Child

Mother & Child

Bully picking on child

Bully picking on child

Bully picking on child

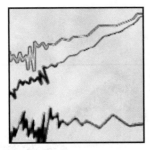

Bird Singing

Rain on Window

Kiss

Mother & Child

Bully picking on a small child

Car Crash

Breaking Glass

Thunder

A Bird Singing

An Upset Stomach

Rain on the Window

Crashing Waves

Tickling

A Kiss

A Blowing Nose

For this activity, you will use all of the elements (line, shape, color, texture, value) to express an idea or concept. Remember what you know about design personality and color psychology. You will be representing a noise or sound using non-representational imagery. Some examples have been provided on this page for you see how to proceed.

Envy

Envy

Tension

Tranquility

Peace

Peace

Anger

Anger

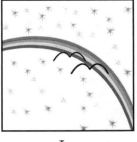

Love

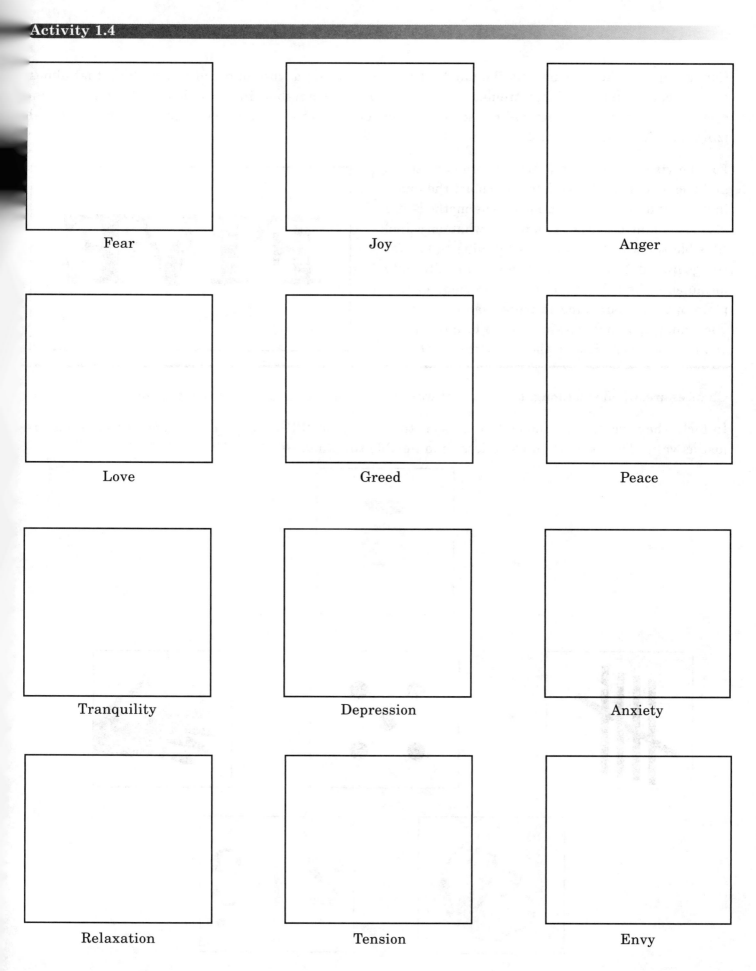

Fear	Joy	Anger
Love	Greed	Peace
Tranquility	Depression	Anxiety
Relaxation	Tension	Envy

II. IDEA GENERATION

Coming up with ideas is usually the toughest part of creating a work of art and something that almos[t] every creative individual has trouble with at one point or another. In the fields of graphic arts, an[d] commercial design, architecture, and so on, the idea or concept is often provided for the artist, but real-izing that idea may be a problem.

For the visual artist, there are numerous methods and tricks that can be used to jump start the imag-ination, and help generate ideas. The methods are also useful in creating a habit of what is called "flexible thinking." This means learning to look at things from different points of view, using alternate formulas to find the solution to a problem, or just plain opening your mind to more than one option. For example, visualize, what comes to mind when you read the word *Five* in the box to the right.

Chances are, when you thought of "FIVE" it was the cardinal numeral seen below, that first came to mind.

In fact, when creating an image to represent the concept of "FIVE," any of the following solutions are just as valid. This is an example of less than flexible thinking.

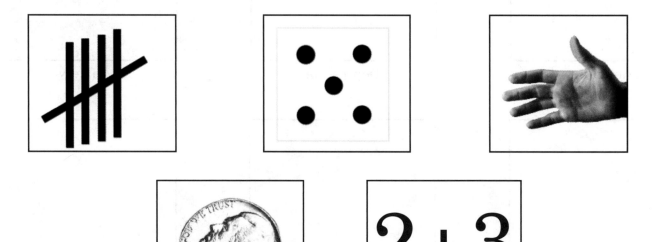

In part two of this Unit, we will examine several ways (by no means all of the ways) of helping to generate ideas or to make your thinking patterns more flexible.

One key component to being more creative or more flexible in your thinking is imagination. Einstein once said "Imagination is more important than intelligence." Einstein, in fact, created his theory of relativity by imagining himself to be a beam of light. Imagination is also a quality or ability everyone has. If you have ever seen animal shapes in the clouds, faces in wood grain, or even the man in the moon, you are using your imagination. In fact, if you can remember what you did yesterday, and can picture yourself doing something else, you are using your imagination.

Being creative is only a matter of learning to use and control your imagination in a constructive way. These exercises should help you to do that.

The first method we will look at is what is called "automatic drawing." This is the very thing you do when you doodle in the margins of your notebook or on a slip of paper while your mind is engaged somewhere else (talking on the phone or watching television for example) and you are not really concentrating on what you're drawing.

Automatic writing was in vogue in the early 1900s and was seen as way for the subconscious to express itself by many prominent psychologists. Needless to say, as a method of "psychoanalysis" it was a tremendous flop. It is, however, an excellent way to jump start the imagination and to force the right hemisphere of the brain (the left side which controls creativity) to begin working.

Activity 2.1—Unconscious Design

Let's begin by trying an activity called a "Free-Doodle." In the space below, randomly scatter a few shapes throughout the area. Now begin to draw lines across the box that move around the shapes, and begin to enclose them or connect them. Keep your lines and line variety constantly changing (thick, thin, close together, far apart).

Let's try a second type of "Free-Doodle." This activity should be done while you are engaged in another activity that doesn't require your full attention (watching television is excellent).

Begin by filling the block below with different lines; thin lines, thick lines, wavy flowing lines, geometric lines that run from edge to edge of the paper. Leave some open spaces between the lines and fill other spaces with textures, values, dots and patterns, etc. Then go back and fill remaining spaces in the same manner.

Remember, the point is to relax and just enjoy the act of filling the page.

We will now move on to an activity called a "Disciplined Doodle." You are going to fill the entire area below with a continuous, single line. You can change the type of line, width or direction. Feel free to leave gaps or create shapes to be filled with tone or pattern later. The only rule is that the initial line must be continuous and unbroken as it twists, doubles back, and winds to fill the given space.

DESIGNING FROM NATURE

Nature and organic forms have provided inspiration and subject matter for artists since the creation of man. Man's earliest works of of art were drawings of animals.

Many artists today still turn to nature for inspiration. Let's take a look at just a few of the ways in which nature can be used to create unique and captivating design.

Many fruits and vegetables when cut in cross sections present the artist with an interesting form. Of course, this needs to be altered by the artist most often by stylization or simplification of what is presented. Below are the examples of natural items that have been simplified to create designs.

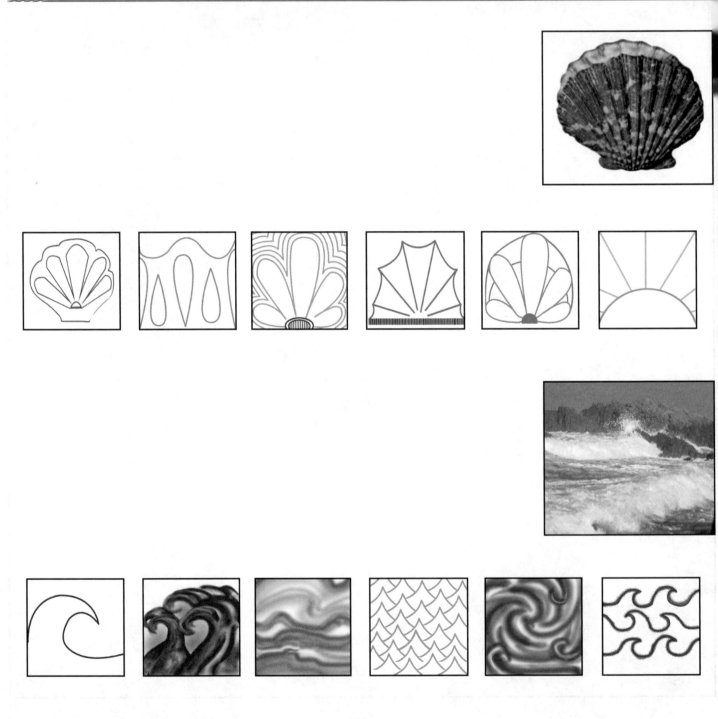

In the large squares below, place three natural objects. You can paste in a picture of an object or draw the object if you can't find a picture. Then create five designs based on the shape, color, and structure of the object. Remember, you are not only creating an attractive or interesting shape, but a well composed design using all you know about principles of design such as, balance, shape, and focal point.

Artists can also create multiple designs from a natural form by cropping the image. Cropping is a term that artists use to refer to cutting off parts of an image or using a portion of the whole to create an interesting image. To easily crop an image, you can use a view finder. Using a razor blade, cut out the square on the next page. Now, find a picture of a plant or flower. Put the picture under the view finder and move the picture around until wha appears inside creates an interesting design Draw what you see in the view finder in the rectangles below. See how many different designs you can create. Try cropping different-sized pictures of the same flower and see what happens

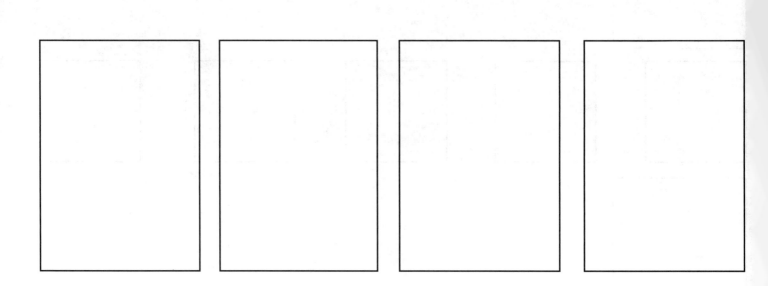

In the row of boxes below, use a picture of a butterfly, grasshopper, spider, or some other insect.

Cut out this
square and use
final product as
your view
finder.

Artists will sometimes make use of an idea generation technique called "Systematic Alteration." This means that an artist can follow a step-by-step procedure to create a design. There are several systems an artist can follow to create such design.

Activity 2.6—Systematic Alteration

To begin, use a technique based on the Punnett square. You will take a sheet of 9 x 12 white construction paper and divide it into 108 one-inch squares by drawing a one-inch grid across the paper. Across the top row, draw a series of simple shapes and again down the left side of the page. You will be creating a new design in each square by combining the two shapes in the square where they intersect. See the square below as an example.

Remember, you can use value, pattern, and texture to add variety and interest to these designs. You are not limited to line only. These designs will probably need to be manipulated a bit to create well composed art, but at least you will have a starting point.

27

Op art, or optical art, was a style of artwork that was devised and became very popular in the mid- to late 1960s. It was very abstract, precise, and geometric. The style was based on the idea of optical illusions and other assorted optical effects, including color vibration and **moiré** effects. Op art used several types of grids to help create interesting compositions. Note the examples below.

©2000 Cordon Art B.V. Baarn Holland, all rights reserved.

M.C. ESCHER'S
METAMORPHOSIS II

Tate Gallery, London.

BRIDGET RILEY'S *MOVEMENT IN SQUARES*

Tate Gallery, London.

BRIDGET RILEY'S *BLAZE 4*

28

ART

Three

UNIT TEST

$\dfrac{36}{44}$

Name_____

Date _____

Score _____

DESIGN PERSONALITY: ART I UNIT THREE TEST

Define the following terms (each answer, 5 points).

1. Analog

    _____

    _____

2. Symbol

    _____

    _____

3. Design Personality

    _____

    _____

4. Automatic Drawing

    _____

    _____

5. Moiré

    _____

    _____

Answer the following questions (each response, 3 points).

6. Describe flexible thinking.

    _____

7. Name one culture besides ours that used grids.

    _____

8. What is the technique where one takes a real object and puts it into an unreal setting?

    _____

9. Explain the difference between a sign, a symbol and an icon (5 points).

    _____

    _____

    _____

    _____

    _____

10. How else, besides design personality, can artwork express ideas? (one way only) (5 points)

_____

_____

One way to create an optical design style is by the use of modules. Modules are design units that can be rearranged in any way to produce an endless variety of patterns that always interlock. The concept is fairly simple. To begin, cut nine squares, each six inches on a side. Make marks below for reference.

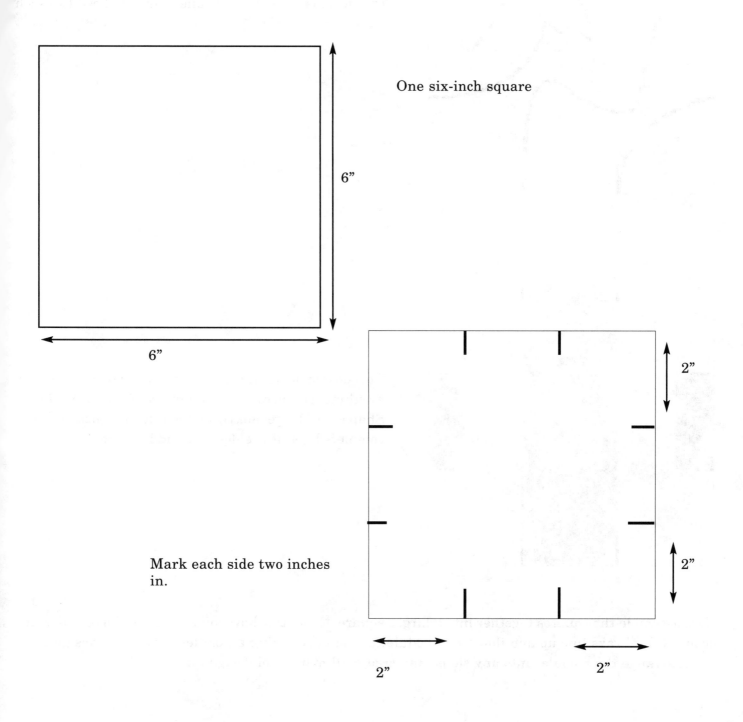

One six-inch square

6"

6"

Mark each side two inches in.

2"

2"

2"

2"

29

The next step is to create a different design on each square. The only requirement is that the design be contained within the two-inch marks on each side (see below).

The designs must be contained within these two-inch lines.

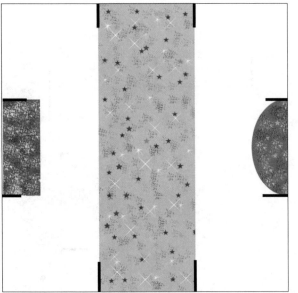

The design motif inside the square can do virtually anything: run across the square, connect, or dead end. Shapes can be geometric or organic in structure. Once completed, paint the designs and background.

Now, assemble the squares together into a larger square. No matter how you rearrange the modules, the design will always line up and flow from module to module, creating an endless variety of designs. You can rearrange the modules into any shape and create all manner of designs.

Yet another way to create an optical style design using the grid is to select a specific number of design units. Then create a grid and fill the grid in a systematic way with the design units. Look at the example below. Go to page 55, cut out all the squares, and place them on the grid.

A

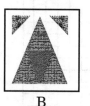

B

C

D

Now, we will create a six-square grid, a seven-square grid, and an eight-square grid. We will create a series of different ways to arrange our units in the grid to create modules.

A	B	C	D	A	B
C	D	A	B	C	D
A	B	C	D	A	B
C	D	A	B	C	D
A	B	C	D	A	B
C	D	A	B	C	D

A	B	C	D	A	B	C
B	B	C	D	A	B	C
C	C	C	D	A	B	C
D	D	D	D	A	B	C
A	A	A	A	A	B	C
B	B	B	B	B	B	C
C	C	C	C	C	C	C

D	A	B	C	C	A	A	D
C	D	A	B	B	B	D	D	C
B	C	D	A	A	C	B	B
A	B	C	D	D	B	C	A
A	B	C	D	D	B	C	A
B	C	D	A	A	C	D	B
C	D	A	B	B	D	A	C
D	A	B	C	C	A	B	D

Now, let's take the six-square grid and place the design units in the proper squares and see what sort of pattern result

					C	D
A	B	C	D	A	B
C	D	A	B	C	D
A	B	C	D	A	B

You can add further variety to your design by altering the shape of the grid or by changing the size and proportions of the individual modules. Take a look at just a few of the possibilities.

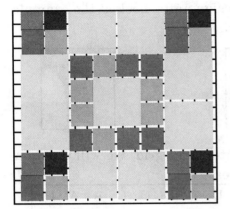 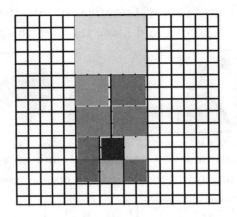 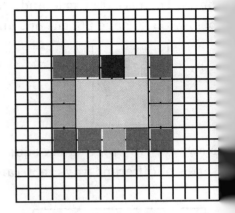

The beauty of the grid is in the fact that it keeps your design unified and at the same time allows for changes in scale, proximity in both positive and negative space.

THE GOLDEN MEAN

There are several other armatures that can be used to help build your design. The oldest is what is known as the *Golden Mean*. Devised by Fra Luca Pacioli in 1509, the Golden Mean is thought to be the "Perfect Proportions." For years artists had been searching for the perfect division of space, since these fundamental proportions had a major impact on how the art work is laid out and composed. The Golden Mean can be represented in many different shapes, from circles to rectangles.

Mathematically, it is the proportion of 1 to 1.618. The Golden Mean is pleasing to the eye because it is *proportionally balanced*. Many architects and artists during the Renaissance used it to achieve a stronger sense of beauty and stability in their work. The Golden Mean can also be seen in nature. It clearly and regularly appears in the growth patterns of many living things, like the spiral formed by a seashell or the curve of a fern.

Draw a square.

Bisect the square. (cut it in half)

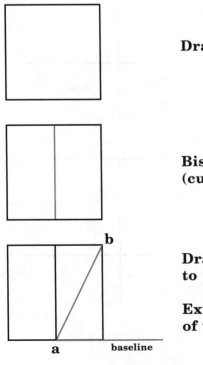

Draw a line from(a) to (b) as shown.

Extend the baseline of the square.

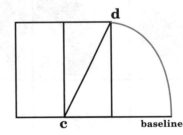

Use a compass. Place the point on (c) and draw an arc from the corner (d), to the baseline.

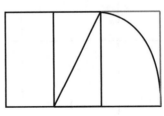

Extend the top and the side lines so they intersect.

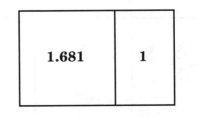

You now have a Golden Mean Rectangle.

One of the interesting things about the Mean is that if you take the last rectangle, divide it in half, divide that half in half, and continue to divide clockwise. Then connect the corners of each division, you will create a nautilus shell spiral.

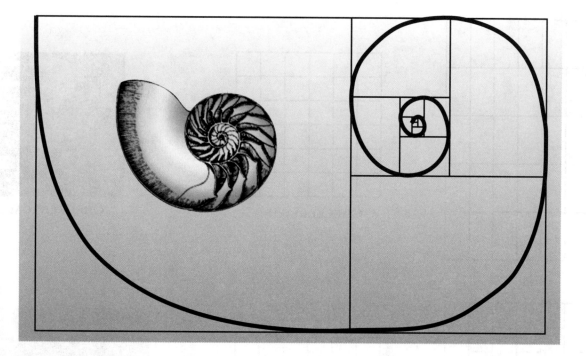

There are several other types of armature that can be used to help create design. This grid is used by Japanese architects in building traditional houses. A Japanese house is built around the size and proportions of the *Tatami*, a straw mat three feet wide by six feet long. The way these mats are laid out in groups determines the size of floors which, in turn, affect the walls. These are basic grids which can be rearranged to create different grid sizes and styles.

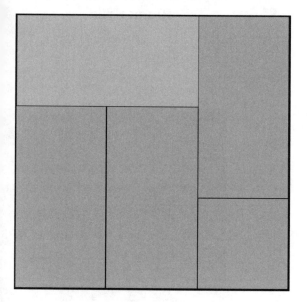

FOUR AND A HALF MATS

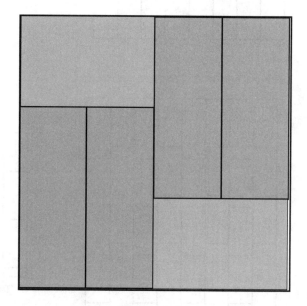

SIX MATS

33

Textile designers have for years, created designs using the grid-based armature. Three such grids are the checkerboard, brick-step, and two third step design. These types of grids are good for creating regular rhythmic or repeating designs. When these designs are regular and become large enough, they create patterns (often used for fabric and wallpaper).

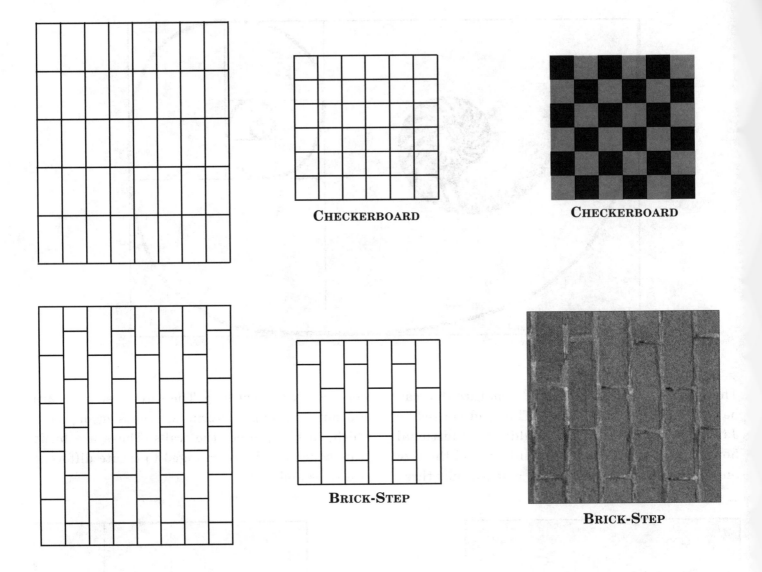

CHECKERBOARD

CHECKERBOARD

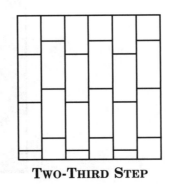

BRICK-STEP

BRICK-STEP

TWO-THIRD STEP

TWO-THIRD STEP

The steps for creating a design using these grids are fairly simple. You begin by making a mark in the first box, then repeat identical marks in each box. In this way you gradually build up a repeating pattern.

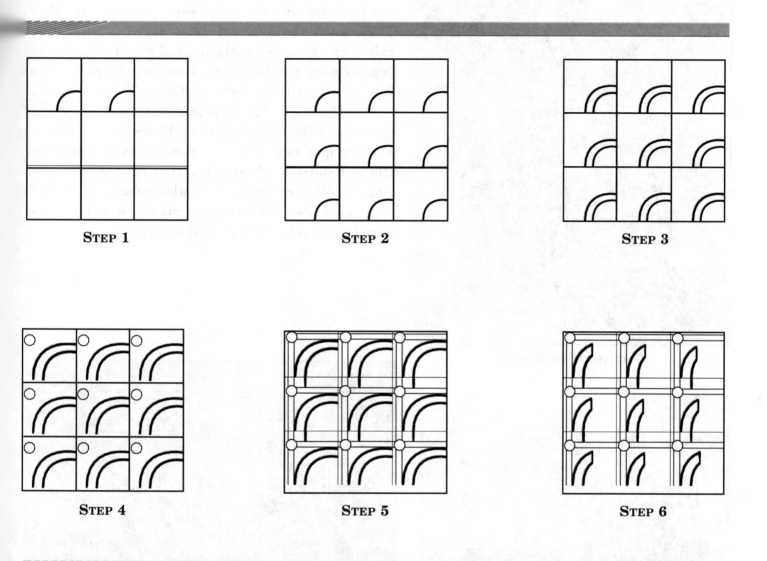

STEP 1

STEP 2

STEP 3

STEP 4

STEP 5

STEP 6

Activity 2.9

You can keep the grid lines or drop them out in the final step. On a piece of 9" x 12" graph paper, draw one of the three types of armature. You may have as many or as few blocks or modules as you like.

Then follow the above steps. When you are finished, erase (or darken) the grid lines and use tempera paint to add color to your design.

HINT—The smaller your modules, the more your design will appear to be a pattern. The larger the modules, the more it will stand on its own.

THE BOOK OF KELLS

CELTIC ART

The ancient **Celts**, who at one time inhabited most of western Europe and the British isles, also used geometry and the grid to create works of art. The Celts had a wonderful artistic style, very graceful and fluid. They filled their artistic objects with decorations called knotting, key patterns, and step patterns. This type of work can be clearly seen in old Celtic manuscripts written by Celtic scribes. Three examples follow. The *Book of Kells* is probably the most famous example of the Celtic artistry. These are illuminated manuscripts depicting the Four Gospels and other Biblical stories. Observe the step pattern and knotting detailing carefully. It is also helpful to research other examples of illuminated manuscripts to see the variety of details evident in the works.

THE BOOK OF KELLS

THE BOOK OF KELLS

To create step patterns, the Celts used a system of dots to create squares which were placed together to form patterns. Let's take a look at how some of these intricate shapes are created. Begin with a "two-square."

Dots are placed at the corners of each square, two long by two high, to create a grid of four total squares.

These dots are then connected to create a design which is repeated in a number of ways.

The more squares, the more complex the design created. One such example is the "three-square."

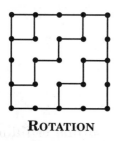

ROTATION

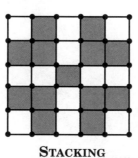

STACKING

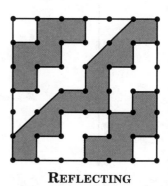

REFLECTING

Look at a few of the ways the squares can be placed together to create interesting patterns. Start with the simple three-square.

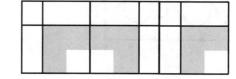

Rows are probably the simplest way to begin.

ROTATION

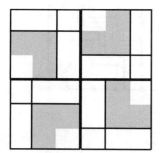

STACKING

REFLECTING

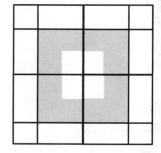

You can also see the use of curves and spirals in the examples on page 36. The basic principle is the same, only the geometric form changes. For example:

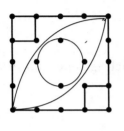

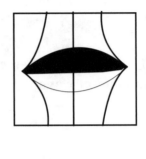
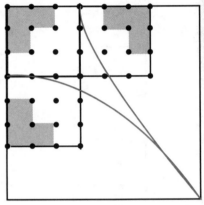

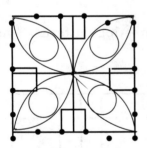

These simple designs can be elaborated on by outline of filling in solid areas of the line.

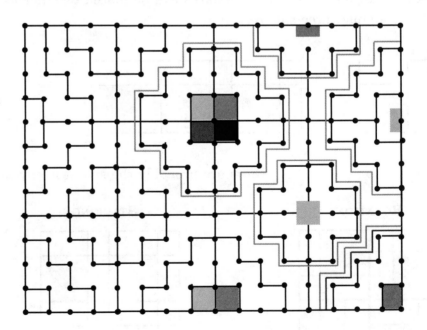

Observe another type of Celtic design work called the *key pattern*. Key patterns are also made by creating a grid of dots, but begin with a set of seven boxes. The lines in a key pattern are drawn in specific order. Try to follow along on a sheet of paper.

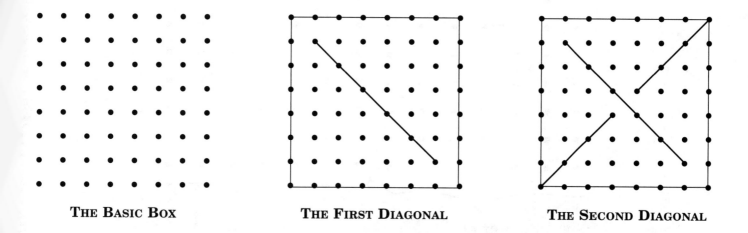

THE BASIC BOX   THE FIRST DIAGONAL   THE SECOND DIAGONAL

The first lines to be drawn are the diagonals, with a diagonal cutting through the middle section, but not touching the corners. The second set runs from corners into the middle at a right angle to the first line, but not touching it.

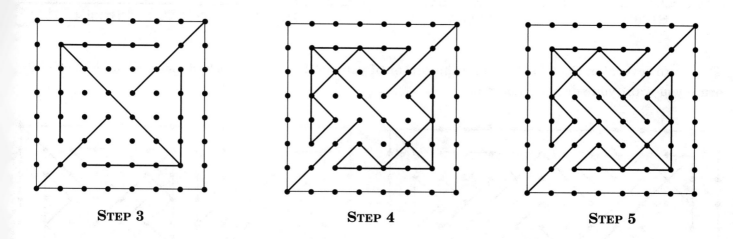

STEP 3   STEP 4   STEP 5

In step three, arrowheads are added to each open corner, again not touching the diagonals. At step four, add a T-shape to each diagonal, and in step five a cross stroke which locks the "key" together. You are creating a sort of a maze design. This design can be grouped together as well create a row or a box as elaborate or simple as you design.

Take a sheet of 9″ x 12″ white construction paper, and follow along to try to lock several keys together.

If you need a reference to draw your grid, put a piece of tissue paper (rather than construction paper) over graph paper and use it as a guide.

These designs are two seven-by-seven keys put together with one row of dots overlapping, creating a series of boxes seven-by-thirteen.

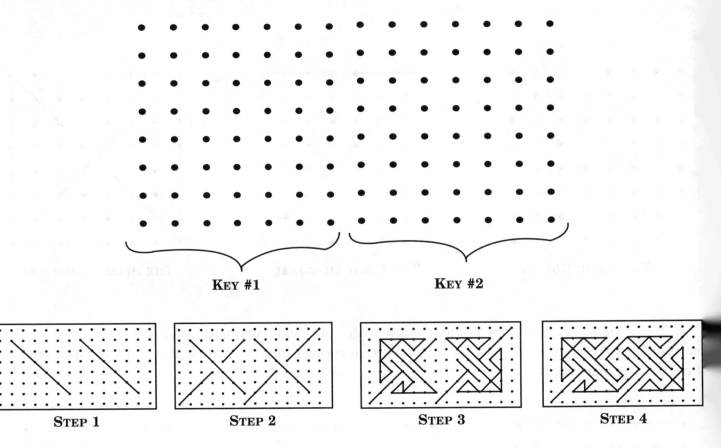

KEY #1   KEY #2

STEP 1   STEP 2   STEP 3   STEP 4

There are several options for finishing the center of your multiple key block, depending upon how elaborate you want your design to become.

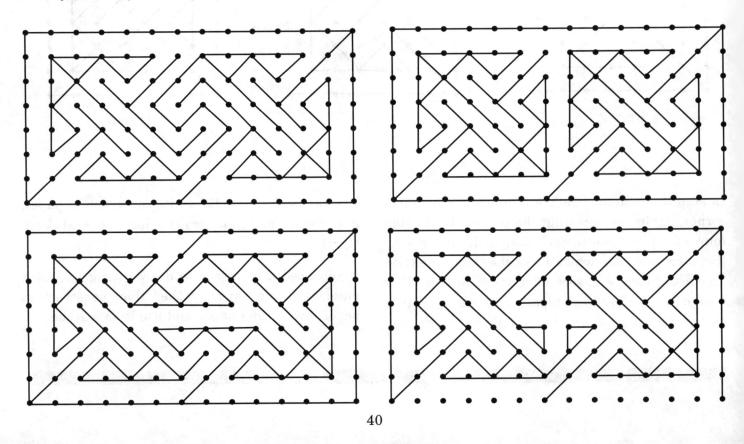

Take a sheet of 9" x 12" white construction paper. Leave at least a one-inch border around the outside edge. Establish a grid of squares inside this border. Feel free to vary the size of the grid squares, the shape of the grid, or maintain a square shape. In the squares below, create at least three design units, and place these in your grid. You may keep the units black and white or use color.

DESIGN UNITS

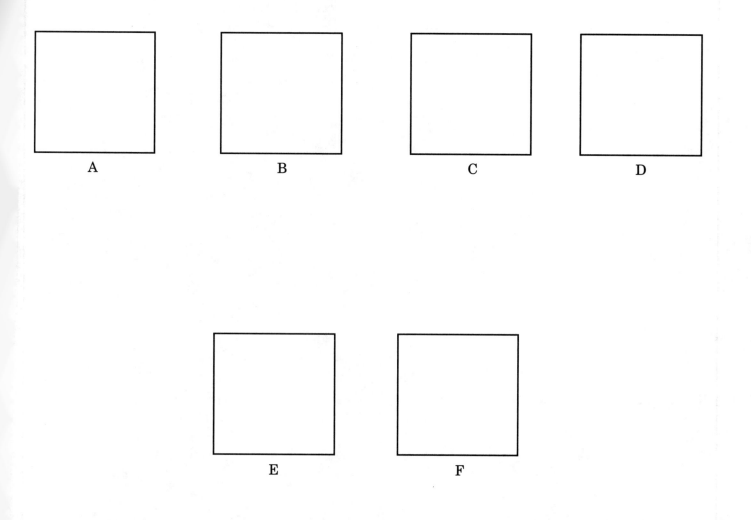

A

B

C

D

E

F

For this activity, you will be using a Celtic technique to create a design. Use a grid for your layout and the techniques learned to create a pattern design. Remember, always consider your composition.

THE GRID

The grid, as well as the use of armature, are two methods that have been used in many cultures as well as in both fine and applied arts.

The world-famous architect Frank Lloyd Wright used the grid as a method for generating designs in floor plans, architecture, and as a method of creating furniture. One can see the geometric applications in his layouts for the building shown below.

He also used the grid to create the following stained glass windows.

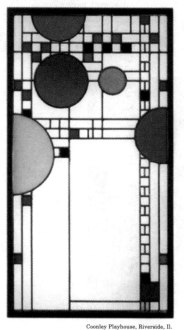

ROBIE HOUSE WINDOW #1,
(1908)*

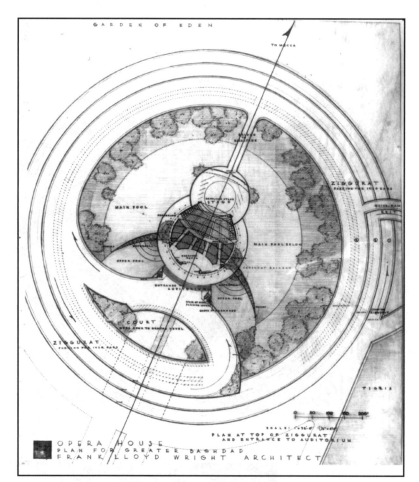

OPERA HOUSE, BAGHDAD*

Lake Geneva Inn, Lake Geneva Wi.

LAKE GENEVA TULIP WINDOW (TOP)
(1911)*

COONLEY PLAYHOUSE,
CLERESTORY #2
(1912)*

* The drawings and window designs of Frank Lloyd Wright are copyright © 2000, the Frank Lloyd Wright Foundation, Scottsdale, Az.

MOIRÉ

Another Op art technique that can be used to create design imagery or structure is called a moiré. This can easily be used in conjunction with any of the doodling techniques discussed earlier. The idea behind a moiré is that when two sets of lines are superimposed at less than 30 degrees the angles create a feeling of vibration or movement similar to that found in color vibration. This effect can take place with any geometric design, but lines work best. Some examples of moiré are shown below.

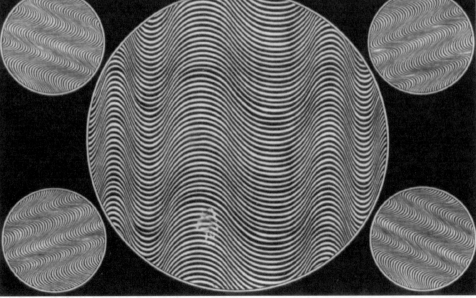

44

Try a moiré of your own. Take a sheet of 9" x 12" paper and draw a one inch border around the edge. To begin, simply draw either a geometric or a wavy line across the paper. Continue to build up additional lines parallel to the first, being sure to keep the distance between the lines, as well as the width of the lines, consistent.

STEP 1

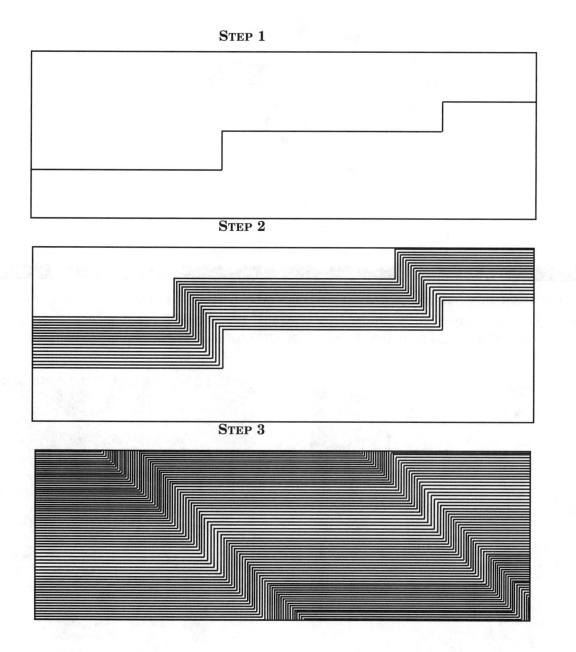

STEP 2

STEP 3

This design by itself will create the illusion of movement at the edges of the lines, and in particular at the corners. To create the moiré, make a second set of lines across the first, at less than the required angle. You will see the moire begin to develop before your eyes.

This design activity will allow you to create an image or pattern using an op art technique in combination with a grid method. This technique allows for a gradual change in either the design unit or the surrounding space, or both, to create the design. It remains unified because the grid keeps the design constant while the units gradually change. In the space below, we can see a simple example of sequential progression in size. Use the grid on page 47 to assist you in creating your design.

In this example, the only change is in size. However, the units could change in shape, or change in both shape and size. Look at the examples below by artist M.C. Escher and see how he has altered the shape gradually. Can you see the layout of the grid? What size and shape is the grid? How does it change in proportion?

©2000 Cordon Art B.V. Baarn Holland, all rights reserved.

M.C. ESCHER'S *BUTTERFLIES*

©2000 Cordon Art B.V. Baarn Holland, all rights reserved.

M.C. ESCHER'S
CREATION OF A METAMORPHOSIS

Use the grid on this page to create a sequential progression design. It's easiest to use a simple shape to begin with. Once the design units are in place, trace the units onto a sheet of 9" x 12" white construction paper, and color in the background, leaving out the grid.

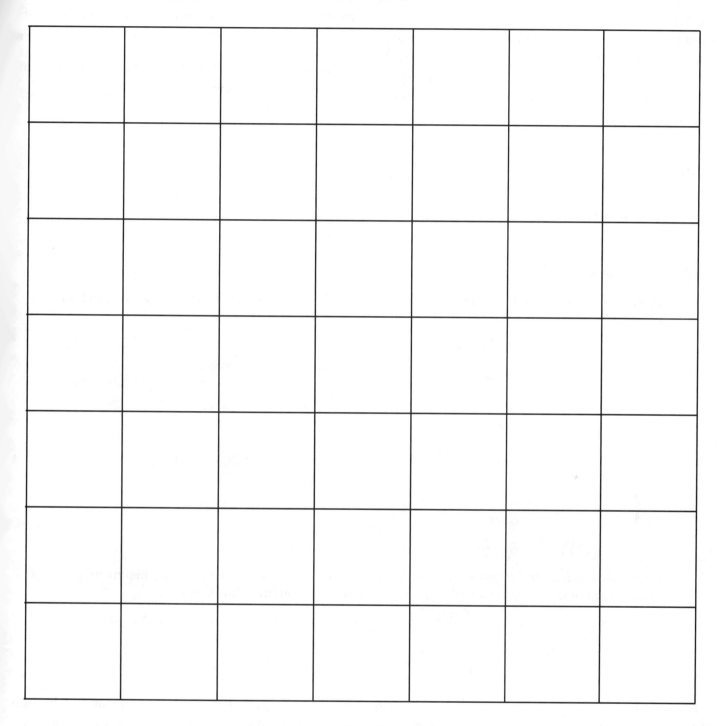

When you have finished your first sequential change, you can begin to create more elaborate designs by varying the proportions of the grid, by varying the shape of the grid, by creating more complex design units, and by concentrating on how the units fit together (the negative space between).

EXPLORATION AND CREATIVE DESIGN

Brainstorming is an approach to the design process in which several people all work together, each contributing ideas while building on comments and suggestions. This is a helpful approach for breaking the barriers in the creative process. Much the same thing can happen by using theme-based idea generation and a technique known as listing and tangents.

Starting with a theme is especially good if you need an idea. However, you need to create subject matter to help realize that idea or give it concrete form.

To create a theme-based design, you must start with a concept, theme, or idea.

EXAMPLE

1. Choose a theme.

EMOTIONS

2. Generate a list of topics related to your theme.

3. Focus on part of your theme and generate another list of ideas, or images related to the theme.

Emotions:

Peace	Heart
Love	Cupid
Anger	Arrows
Envy	Arrow through a heart
Joy	
Greed	
Sympathy	

4. Now you have a list of possible subject matter to be used to create your design or piece of artwork, as well as several techniques to use for structuring that design.

Listing and tangents lead us to an area of design communication where the subject matter speaks directly to the viewer. Extracting meaning directly from the subject matter is called *symbolism*.

Signs and symbols are interpretations of human experience. We all deal with symbols on a daily basis, from traffic lights to street signs to restroom doors. Most people are very adept at reading or interpreting signs and symbols.

Design by accident is an additional way for the artist to create artwork and design and break through the mental blocks that sometimes make it difficult to generate ideas.

Design by accident can also be a fun way to play with various media and enjoy the discovery process. Many artists have used this technique to great effect. In particular was the surrealist Max Ernst.

Surrealism is a technique or style in which the artist takes a real object and puts it into an unreal setting to create a dreamlike image. Ernst used many techniques but was well known for what is called **frottage** or rubbing or pressing together.

By applying paint to a surface and then applying force, the paint could be textured or squeezed into unique shapes. Ernst would then use these shapes to create surreal images by turning them into landscapes or figures.

Observe the following example and see if you can pick out the textured areas.

©2000, Artists Rights Society (ARS), New York/ADAGP, paris.

MAX ERNST'S *EVERYONE HERE SPEAKS LATIN*

DESIGN ACTIVITIES

Activity 2.14

There are many techniques to create design using frottage. The first, and most well-known, will create a non-representational design similar to those you see in the Rorshach ink blot test (commonly used by psychologists).

To experiment with this technique, fold a 9" x 12" sheet of white construction paper in half. Now, dribble a bit of tempera paint onto one side of the paper, fold it over and press down on it. When you open the paper you will see a perfectly symmetrical design.

Try this experiment with colored tempera on black paper as well.

You can experience a different type of frottage by taking a piece of glass and using several different colors, dribble some tempera on the glass. Take a sheet of construction paper and press it down onto the glass. When you pull it off the glass, you will see a textured design. You can create different textures by waiting and allowing the paint to dry or applying different amounts of pressure to the paper as well.

You can create yet another texture by watering down the tempera and painting it generously on a piece of construction paper. Now take a piece of plastic wrap, crumple it up and lay it down on the wet paint. When the paint is dry, peel off the plastic wrap and examine the texture.

While the textures can be quite enjoyable to create, they can also be used to create quite interesting compositions.

Examine the Ernst painting. Can you see the figures and the landscapes in them? Do you see buildings? Ernst has created just enough image so you can pick other things out of the texture.

Examine texture—scan anything be seen in them? Working with a pencil, paint, or by cutting areas away, try to create an image from the textures.

Try cutting some shapes out of the texture and glue them down to a neutral background color. Can you create a cityscape or landscape? With this end result in mind, try to create new frottage and control the texture for your use.

Designing by accident can be quite enjoyable and sometimes just what it takes to juggle the imagination enough to get some good creative thoughts running through your head.

Try several different methods for creating some interesting looking designs and textures.

Activity 2.15

Spread some newspaper down across a table.

Take a sheet of 9" x 12" construction paper and crumple it loosely into a ball, then flatten it out again. Iron if needed to smooth it out. Rub the surface with a piece of carbon paper to see what surface texture it reveals.

Try the same experiment using a piece of tracing paper, regular writing paper, and other sorts of paper.

Activity 2.16

For this activity, take a shallow cup of water and place it on top of a sheet of 9" x 12" construction paper. Pour some india ink into the water. (Make sure there are several layers of newspaper under the construction paper) put a straw into the water and blow bubbles until they overflow onto the paper. If the water does not bubble enough, just add some dishwashing detergent.

When the bubbles spill over onto the paper, allow them to spread out and dry.

Take a sheet of 9" x 12" construction paper and wet it under running water. When it is totally wet, lay it flat on several layers of newspaper. Using the dropper in the bottle, drop India ink, one drop at a time, onto the paper. Allow drops to spread out and dry.

This is a classic design by accident experiment. If you have crayons, take a knife or a vegetable peeler and scrape several shavings onto a piece of construction paper. Place another piece of paper on top and iron on medium to high setting until all the pieces are melted. Quickly peel apart the two pieces of paper before the wax cools. What sort of surface appearance do you have?

This activity is similar to your first experiment in frottage. Take a sheet of paper and fold it in half. Now, take several pieces of string and paint each one a different color. Place the string on the piece of paper and fold it over. Putting pressure onto the paper sandwich, pull out the string. Open the paper to see what you have.

For this activity, you will need a box. Place a sheet of paper on the bottom of the box. Take round objects, a golf ball, ping pong ball, stones or marbles and roll them in paint. Put these in the box and roll them around to see what sort of textures they produce. Try using different color papers and different color paints.

These last few activities are not meant to create great works of art, but just encourage exploration of possibilities, especially when you are having a hard time coming up with ideas.

By now, you should be able to see how these techniques might be incorporated into your artwork.

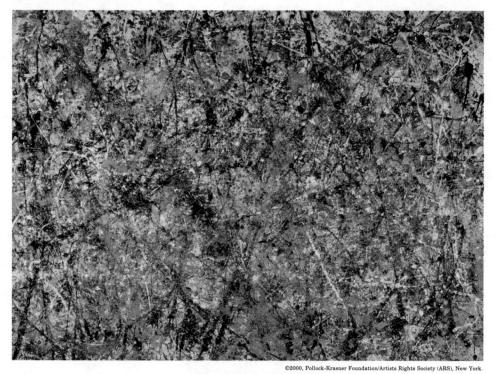

©2000, Pollock-Krasner Foundation/Artists Rights Society (ARS), New York.

JACKSON POLLOCK'S *LAVENDER MIST*

EVALUATION

Now that you have completed *Design Personality*, it is time to look at what you have learned. Glanc
back at your original expectations. Did you learn or encounter what you expected
Was the Unit different, and if so, how?

_____

_____

_____

_____

_____

_____

Try to think of at least three new things you were exposed to in the Unit, and explain them here as i
you had to explain them to someone who is unfamiliar with this Unit.

What do you think is the most important thing you have gleaned from this Unit?

_____

_____

_____

_____

_____

_____

_____

_____

_____

_____

_____

_____

_____

GLOSSARY

Analog—A symbol or item which represents or stands for something else.

Armature — Structure or supporting structure something is built on.

Celts—(pronounced *Kelts*) A group of people who inhabited most of western Europe (Gaul), prior to the Roman invasions

Frottage —Rubbing or pressing two or more things together.

Geometric—Pertaining to geometry, it's methods and principles.

Icon—An icon is a symbol which has direct resemblance to the concept or item it represents.

Inorganic—Man-made

Moiré —An independent, shimmering pattern seen when two geometrically regular patterns are superimposed, especially at acute angles.

Organic—Having to do with, or coming from nature.

Signs—Signs are visual symbols that stand for something. They convey complex and large amounts of information in a simple and direct way.

Symbol—A symbol is an image that conveys meaning indirectly; it represents an idea but may not look like or have anything to do with what it represents.

Textile —Having to do with cloth or fabric.

Before taking the Unit Test, you may want to do one or more of these self checks.
1. _____ Read the objectives. Check to see if you can do them.
2. _____ Restudy the material related to any objectives that you cannot do.
3. _____ Use the SQ3R study procedure to review the material.
4. _____ Review activities, Self Tests, and Unit vocabulary words.
5. _____ Restudy areas of weakness indicated by the last Self Test.

A

B

C

D

A

B

C

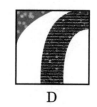

D

A

B

C

D

A

B

C

D

A

B

C

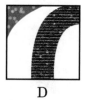

D

56

57